Preface

While there are rituals and ceremonies for birth, marriage, and death, there are few for separation and divorce. With no "procedures" to follow, and many emotional, social, financial, and legal pressures to face, families are often left feeling isolated and helpless.

Every family is unique; each has its own identity or personality. Yet, families who have separated or divorced share many common concerns. These concerns and the struggle to resolve them form the basis of this book.

The National Family Resiliency Center, Inc was developed to help children and families adjust to separation and divorce in healthy ways. The center is supported through grants, individual and corporate contributions, and fees for service.

Most of the families who utilize NFRC services live in Howard and Montgomery counties, Maryland. However, we feel safe in predicting that no matter where you may live, your experiences as a separated or divorced parent are similar to those described in this handbook. Our goal is threefold: to convey to you that you are not alone, to provide you with positive ways of coping with problems related to separation and divorce, and to discuss ways in which you can help your children.

This book is dedicated to the multitude of children and families who struggle to adjust to separation and divorce. We give special thanks to the almost 18,000 individuals who have participated in our center, who opened up their world of feelings, who coped with a stressful event in their lives, and who have gone on with a sense of hope and a new sense of family.

Our thanks go as well to our families and to the staff and peer counselors at the Naional Family Resiliency Center, Inc., for their love, support, and encouragement.

Risa Garon LCSW-C, BLD, CFLE
Executive Director & Co-Founder

Barbara Mandell R.N., M.A., C.S.-P
Co-Founder

D1283299

Contents

Introduction

Some people think of separation and divorce as the end of a family. In this handbook, we take a different view: we see separation and divorce as a process of adjustment, involving choices and changes.

The marriage is ended, but the family continues to exist in a restructured and more complex form. Husband and wife, though physically separated, continue as parents of their children, but must adjust to being single parents or not seeing their children on a daily basis. Children continue to need their parents' guidance and support, but must adapt to separate households and scheduled time with parents.

The choices and changes families must make present opportunities to learn from the past, take risks, and grow.

The following chapters describe the common reactions and changes that occur after a separation and divorce. Each chapter includes several tasks, or concrete suggestions, for parents to use as they help their children adjust to a new family situation.* Some of the tasks are best accomplished individually with each child, one on one; others are best done with both, or all, of your children, together. The approach you take depends on your children's ages, personalities, levels of maturity, as well as the task itself.

These tasks require effort and courage. Experience has proven that these efforts have immediate and long-term benefits not only for children, but for the entire network of family relationships.

Throughout the handbook we refer to "your child" alternately as she and he.

Chapter 1

Explaining Separation and Divorce to Children

Many parents say that telling their children about their intention to separate or divorce is the most painful thing they've ever had to do. Parents anticipate and fear the hurt their children will experience and blame themselves for inflicting this hurt. Some parents think their children aren't emotionally strong enough to hear the truth; other parents are so shocked by an unexpected separation that they cannot find the words or strength to tell their children. Tensions run high between spouses at this time, and parents may hope to avoid an argument by not explaining their plans for a divorce.

Difficult as it may be, it is very important to talk to your children about the separation or divorce—be open and honest and include them in your discussions. This helps children make sense of a very confusing situation. In preparing yourself for this difficult task, the experience of others may serve as a guide.

- Time and again, children state that they want the "honest truth." Children often know more than their parents think about the problems underlying the separation or divorce. Openly sharing what may have already been suspected may be very sad, but may also bring a sense of relief. Children often say: "I knew it was coming. I wasn't surprised."

- Other children have little idea of their parents' problems and express a wish that they had been warned before the separation. Still others first learn of a separation when they see a parent moving out of the house. In general, children who are not given adequate warning and explanation see themselves as having been left out and deprived of control. Years later, they may experience a sense of hurt, resentment, and confusion.

- Children may be too young to understand much of what is explained to them. However, they will retain some memory of what has been said, and this can be built upon as they get older and want more information.

- Parents who sit down together with their children and discuss what has happened are giving their children a reassuring message: we both take responsibility for handling this situation and your future. Parents who are willing to talk, cry, and express feelings, are inviting their children to be open and honest about the separation and all other areas of their lives.

- When children realistically understand the reason for a separation or divorce, they can:

  - feel relieved of the guilt that can result from thinking they may have caused their parents' problems

  - reduce the anger which results from thinking that their parents behaved "badly"

  - have a realistic view of their parents as human beings with strengths and weaknesses

- understand interpersonal relationships and be better prepared for relationships of their own.

Ideally, both parents should sit down together and tell children about the separation before it happens. However, if this joint discussion cannot occur, one parent can communicate with the child and work on the following tasks in a caring, comprehensive way.

TASKS

1. Give explanations which indicate that it takes two to create marital dissatisfaction. Example: "Daddy had many friends and activities outside the home. I wanted more time together."

2. Comment on your spouse's behavior; don't judge or condemn your spouse (the human being.) Avoid exaggerations or generalizations. Example: "Mommy drinks more than I would like her to" rather than "Mommy is a drunk."

3. Help your child see that the marriage brought happiness as well as difficulties. This perspective will help your child accept the fact that as time passed, the needs of one or both parents could no longer be satisfied by the marriage, causing frustration and conflict. Explain that you and your ex-spouse were not able to fix the problems that developed. Acknowledge that some problems cannot be fixed.

4. Gear the conversation to your child's age and level of understanding.

   Preschool children need concrete information about how their daily routines will be affected. They will need to know details, such as when they will see each parent and who will care for them during certain times of the day. It can be helpful to use story-writing, drawing, doll-play, and reading as tools for communicating information to your young child and exploring his reactions.
   Like pre-schoolers, elementary school aged children need specific information about the impact of separation on their lives. When will

they see each parent? Where will they live? Will they continue to attend the same school?

Elementary schoolers are particularly concerned with the question of who is responsible for the marital difficulties. They need to be reassured that they did not (and cannot) cause or remedy parental problems, that they need not decide if one parent is right, and that they are free to have a continued loving relationship with each parent.

Pre-adolescent and older children need additional information about marital relationships, between their parents and between adults in general. They need to understand what determines the success of a relationship and what particular factors affected development of their parents' relationship over the years. This information is essential to allay their anxiety about possibly entering into marriage without proper preparation and having the marriage end in divorce.

You might sit down with your older child and discuss aspects of your marital relationship in an objective manner. Share how each spouse changed over time and how the changes affected the marriage. Explaining how each spouse coped with the problems will help your child begin to distinguish between solvable and unsolvable problems or differences. An example might be : "When your father and I first got married, I wanted to stay home and have a family. As I got older I realized I wanted to return to school and establish a career. Your father resented my leaving home, and we had a lot of arguments which we never resolved. We grew in different ways and tried to compromise, but I couldn't stay home full time the way your father wanted me to."

5. Expect your child to ask the same questions repeatedly and to ask new questions as they get older. It takes time for a child to digest the information you provide and to accept the reality of the situation.

Chapter 2

Common Reactions to Separation and Divorce

The period before and after a separation or divorce can be a time of emotional turmoil for parents and children. While there may be relief from years of conflict and pain, and hope for a better future, there is also a strong sense of hurt and loss.

Many people compare their response to separation or divorce to the grieving process that follows death. It involves reactions of shock or disbelief, anxiety, anger, sadness, guilt and acceptance. These reactions do not necessarily occur in a particular order, nor do they last for a set period of time. Grieving may actually begin before the separation has actually occurred; it may occur when the separation has been anticipated.

The stage of acceptance is often the most difficult to achieve. With death, there is a final loss, and one is able to come to grips with the fact that the lost one is not returning. With separation and divorce, however, one or both parents may come and go in the life of the child. There may be unrealistic, but ongoing, longing for an absent parent or spouse and a continuous need to adapt to changes in relationships.

The following pages describe some of the common reactions to separation and divorce.

Shock or Disbelief

Parents describe a sense of confusion or a dazed feeling, as if they are only going though the motions of living. Both parents and children may act as if nothing has changed—e.g., by not telling friends or neighbors about the separation. Children may fantasize about a reunited family or may attempt to bring parents together by misbehaving or becoming ill.

Parents may say to themselves, This can't be happening, it's a temporary stage my spouse is going through; this will not last. Children may be thinking, Maybe if I don't think about this, it won't be true.

Anxiety

For both parents and children, there is a great deal of concern about present and future survival. Anxiety can make it difficult to concentrate at work or school
and can lead to minor disturbances in sleep, appetite, and physical well-being.

Parents wonder: How will I cope? It will be terribly hard to make it on my own. Can I do it? How will I tolerate the difficulties and the loneliness?

Children worry: What will happen to me? Will both parents still love and take care of me? How will others treat me when they find out my parents are separated or divorced? Was it my fault?

Anger

Both parents and children feel angry that a divorce has happened to them. Often, that anger is manifested by a short temper, lowered tolerance of frustration, and more rigid expectations of oneself and others.

Adults may find it difficult to refrain from blaming their ex-spouse, and children may blame one or both parents for the divorce. Children may become less cooperative at home and at school and may be more prone to conflicts with family members and peers.

A parent's reaction may be: This shouldn't be happening to me. Life is too hard. Everything is ruined. It's not fair. My ex-spouse had no right to do this. Children may react similarly: My parents had no right to do this to one another and me; they should have known better.

Sadness

It is natural for parents and children to feel a deep sense of sadness following separation or divorce. This sadness is associated with a sense of loss; for parents, the loss of a loving relationship; for children, a partial and sometimes complete loss of contact with a parent. For both parents and children, there is the loss of the routines, events, and happy occasions associated with the family as it once was. Finally, there is the loss of family plans, hopes and dreams for the future.

At first, it is especially difficult to recognize that life can go on happily in the future. The sadness of loss is deepened by worries about the future. Adults may think: If this relationship has failed, perhaps I may never find someone to love and care for me; if I do not, I may never by happy.

Guilt

Parents may blame themselves because they believe that they have failed in their marriage, and have created unpleasant circumstances, particularly for their children. Parents who experience guilt find it more difficult to be attentive to their own needs and to behave assertively with ex-spouses or with their children. A sense of guilt is created by thoughts such as: Look what I've done...how terrible of me.

Children may believe that they have created or contributed to their parents' problems. This belief is reinforced when parents fight over visits, expenses, or other child-related issues. When children experience a sense of self blame and guilt, they, too, may find it difficult to be assertive in satisfying their needs. They may become over-protective of their parents, or in some cases may misbehave to be punished for their imagined wrong-doings.

Acceptance

A sense of acceptance occurs when parents and children recognize that there is a new life beyond separation and divorce. Parents realize, I can accept myself and others and my life as it is, and may view the future as an opportunity for greater happiness and satisfaction. They are able to establish new goals and interests, new relationships outside the family, and a stronger support network of community, professional, or religious ties.

While children rarely give up the wish that their parents will reunite, they may reach a point where they can relate to one or both parents with a sense of security, satisfaction, and confidence that they are loved. Children can finally admit, I still wish my parents were together, but I can be happy anyway. They re-establish outside interests, close relationships with family and friends, and involvement with school work.

TASKS

1. Accept that after a separation or divorce, you and your child will have strong feelings. As time passes, these feelings will become less painful. Meanwhile, however, your child needs reassurance that disclosing true feelings will not hurt or anger you. Communicating is an effective way for you and your child to solve problems and deal with emotions.

    It is difficult for parents to tune into their child's feelings because it reminds them of the pain the child has had to endure. But ignoring these feelings will only prolong, rather than lessen, your child's pain. If you and your child become overwhelmed by emotions, it will be hard for you to communicate, problem solve, and support one another.

2. Let your child know that you are interested and willing to talk about thoughts and feelings. Set aside a special time for sharing. If you are a person who holds in your own feelings, it may require effort on your part to serve as an example for your child. However, avoid burdening your child. The purpose of these conversations is to help your child. It is important that you, as a parent, seek understanding and support from other adults.

    You might sit down on your child's bed or take a walk and say: "I know these last few weeks have been hard for all of us. I've felt sad; other times angry; other times relieved. I think it's important for us to share and understand each other's feelings. I know it's scary, and you may worry about hurting me. But feelings are neither right or wrong, and you will only help me by letting me know what you're feeling. We may have some of the same feelings. Let's try, okay?"

3. Do not try to talk your child out of feeling a certain way. Let your child know that his feelings are accepted and understood. A wish that Mommy and Daddy will go back together may be unrealistic and impractical, but is nonetheless quite normal.

4. Try to correct ideas that may be causing your child to be unnecessarily upset. For example, your children may incorrectly blame one parent for problems in the marriage and feel unduly angry or may blame themselves and feel guilty. Let your children know that it is all right to ask questions about the separation or divorce and about what will happen in the future. Listen and answer the questions honestly.

5. Try to understand your own thoughts, feelings, and behavior and how they affect your child. If you communicate extreme hopelessness, anger, anxiety, or guilt, your child may react to these emotions.

    Again, it is very important for you to have other adults to turn to so that your child will not be bombarded with extreme anger or other emotions. At the same time, for your sake, it is important to assess whether the extreme emotion is going to help or harm you. You may find that the same amount of energy spent being angry, can be used to plan something constructive in your life that will bring you happiness.

6. If a situation is upsetting your child, help your child problem solve by discussing possible alternatives. For example, children who miss an absent parent can learn to express this feeling, and request more time together in a non-blaming way. Ways to remain close might include phone calls, letters, tapes, or diaries.

7. Encourage your child to associate with others who have experienced separation and divorce and to read related books by or for children. This will help your child see that other children feel the same way that they do.

8. Make a point of sharing happy thoughts and feelings with your child. This will help her realize that separation and divorce do not signify failure and that life can be filled with success and satisfaction.

Chapter 3

Handling Changes In Family Relationships

Many relationships change as a result of separation and divorce. Sometimes these changes involve separation, not only from a parent, but also from brothers and sisters, grandparents and other extended family members, neighbors, and friends. Separation and divorce also introduce children to new relationships with their parents' friends, new spouses, and stepfamily. The greatest changes, however, occur between parents and children.

Parents, particularly those who are not involved with their child on a daily basis, feel like they have lost a substantial part of their identity. Parents who are "twenty-four-hour-a-day parents" report that they miss spending pleasurable time with their child, and have to scramble just to get a few moments of sharing.

Communication, time together, and discipline are all affected by separation and divorce. Time together may be limited and feel awkward. Parents wonder how to restart a relationship when they don't see or communicate with a child daily. Parents who do have daily access to their child wonder how much they should share their feelings or respond to their child's expressed or internalized feelings. Parents may, for the first time, be developing a close relationship with their child and don't want to risk alienating them by enforcing rules. Discipline often becomes lax because parents do not want to put any additional burden on their children; some parents feel that they don't want to discipline their child when they are not spending a lot of time together.

Children need to be nurtured and guided by each parent. This may not be possible in all family situations. In striving to build healthy parent-child relationships, parents need to spend unconditionally loving time with their child, talk to, and listen to them. Children need help in learning to express their feelings and practicing problem solving. Parents need to guide children with rules and consequences that will help them behave appropriately, learn right from wrong, and exercise healthy self control.

TASKS

1. Maintain open communication with your child. By dealing directly with painful feelings and problems, you will both be less likely to resort to frequent yelling, hitting, or other methods of acting out feelings.

2. Listen carefully to your child's thoughts and feelings. If your child requests a change (in your behavior, in a routine, etc.) and the request is reasonable and possible, do it. Correct any misconceptions your child may have, but do not attempt to judge or take away feelings. Those feelings belong to your child.

3. Be open and honest with your child when evaluating the quality and amount of time you spend together. Do not allow a sense of guilt or protectiveness to prevent either of you from taking time alone. On the other hand, if there does not seem to be enough shared time, prioritize your commitments and carve out time to spend together in a way you both enjoy. Your child will benefit from special time with one or both parents.

4. Plan your time in advance and in writing. This action will increase your commitment. It will enable you and your child to make the most of your

time together, and allow you to plan enjoyable activities to do alone or with others when you and your child are apart.

5. Work out logistics very specifically. Older children should participate in planning time with each parent. Younger children need help making plans. When your child doesn't live with you on a daily basis, arrange specific, scheduled phone calls and visits, and keep your commitment to your child. If you cannot do this, let your child know why. Missed visits should not become a habit because they may create anxiety for your child, and he may view this as a rejection or an indication that you do not care.

6. Expect some awkwardness when you see or speak to your child after being apart. It is hard to get started. You might:

    •   Include your child in discussing your schedule of phone calls and time together;

    •   Allow your child to talk about what he wants to do and who he would like to include. A calendar for each of you can be helpful.

    •   Spend some time alone with your child during each visit. Children need concrete reassurance that they maintain a special place with their parent, even if the parent has remarried or lives with someone.

7. Try to have a natural relationship even though time is condensed. Plan activities together; but save time for relaxing and talking together at home. Attend and participate in your child's important events at school and other places. If you keep up with current activities, you are more apt to be informed about future dates and events. Write them down and double check dates and times with your child's other parent.

8. Allow your child to continue with the important activities in her life. There will be times when your child will have a birthday party or soccer game to attend when she is supposed to be spending time with you. If you understand that this is part of your child's life, and do not view it as a rejection, your child will be less likely to feel guilty.

9. Provide some space (a drawer, closet, room) and keep some personal possessions (stuffed animals, toys, books, clothes) for your child at both homes.

10. Try to have clearly stated rules and mutually agreed upon chores. Maintaining structure emphasizes the continued parenting aspect of the relationship.

11. Many times children will complain to one parent about spending time with the other. Encourage your child to discuss his concerns directly with the parent involved; to say to that parent, "I was really looking forward to you picking me up at noon, and when you didn't show up, I felt hurt and disappointed." In order to do this, your child may need help practicing how to approach your former spouse.

Children's Loyalty to Both Parents

Children want to love, respect, and be loyal to both parents. Your child's ability to maintain a sense of loyalty depends upon:

- the way in which you and your former spouse make decisions about living arrangements, child care costs, and your child's needs. When old conflicts are played out during the planning process, children are deprived of a model of effective negotiations. Children may assume an inappropriate involvement in the decision-making process to protect their parents from this unpleasant experience, and even attempt to ensure that their needs will be met.

- the extent to which you and your former spouse speak in angry, blaming terms about one another. Children often feel hurt for the parent being harshly criticized and resentful of the highly critical parent. They may assume a protective stance toward one or both parents.

- the degree to which you and your ex-spouse question your child about each other's lives. Some children feel caught in the middle when one parent questions them about who the other parent is dating, or gives them messages to deliver to the other parent.

- the degree to which the child is free to ask questions, comment about situations which cause him discomfort, and request change.

- the general well being of both parents. Children are often highly protective of parents who are depressed, withdrawn, or in some way severely suffering because of the separation or divorce.

TASKS

1. Put aside old conflicts when planning for your child. Avoid using time with your children or money as a weapon. If your ex-spouse chooses to do so, share your sense of frustration and disappointment with your child without totally condemning the other parent.

2. Avoid placing your child in situations where she must choose between you and your ex-spouse. Consult your child about her feelings and preferences concerning such things as living arrangements or time together, but maintain control when determining what is best.

3. Avoid "blowing off steam" about your ex-spouse in your child's presence. Rely on friends or seek professional counseling to deal with feelings of extreme anger or frustration. However, do not go to the opposite extreme and make excuses for a parent's behavior. Help your child see that the parent has a mixture of qualities—strengths and weaknesses. Focus on the behavior. Do not condemn the individual.

4. Respect the other parent's privacy and your child's right to relax and enjoy time with the parent without having to "report back."

5. Communicate directly with your ex-spouse. If this is not possible, use another adult; do not use your child as a messenger.

6. Encourage your child to comment and ask questions about his relationships with you and his other parent. By doing so, you are demonstrating a willingness to listen, respect of your child's feelings, and ability to make changes when appropriate.

Children and Stepfamily Relationships

It is very important to discuss the decision to remarry with children. Children need to talk about their reactions and to hear from their parent that they are still loved and will spend time together.

Remarriage almost always results in a time of confusion and concern for children. How will they be treated by their stepparent? What should they call him/her? If they like their stepparent, does this mean they are being disloyal to their biological parent, or will this hurt the parent's feelings?

Stepparents, too, may be confused at times. When do they discipline? How are they referred to in public? Are they invited and expected to attend school conferences or other activities?

The stepparents need time to develop as a couple and freedom to participate in activities as a couple. They must also contend with an "instant family." Before a remarriage, both partners need to thoroughly discuss parenting—what they expect from one another and from the children, how they will discipline and what rules will be followed. Clearly defining rules and boundaries prevents children from being put in the middle, or putting either parent in the middle.

TASKS

1. Let your child decide what she feels comfortable calling a stepparent and vice versa. Let the stepparent and child decide together how they would like to be addressed in public.

2. Convey positive expectations of your new marriage and new stepfamily. As a couple, share time, friends, and activities apart from the children. Also share family times and activities together on a regular basis.

3. Clearly communicate rules and consequences. Hold family discussions to make decisions about issues such as chores. Let the child know in what areas he can have input and in what areas he cannot. Allow time for working out specific situations or problems as they arise.

4. Recognize that there is enough of your child's love for everyone—-even stepparents. Sometimes a stepparent can become a special friend by

diffusing anger between ex-spouses or between a parent and child. A new stepparent may want to meet the ex-spouse to discuss ways to better understand and be more helpful to the stepchild.

5.   Help your child express her anxious, angry, confused, or loving feelings toward her stepparent and step siblings. Be aware that it may be difficult for your child to share you with your new partner and your partner's children. She may also have difficulty with the loss of status as youngest or oldest child. Help your child express feelings of confusion, anxiety, or anger. Make sure to spend time alone with your child to minimize her sense of loss. Help your child discuss and generate alternative solutions for difficulties she may have with her step siblings. Give the children time to establish step sibling bonds.

6.   Help your child gradually become acquainted with new relatives. A new stepfamily affords children an opportunity to form satisfying relationships with extended kin. Discuss how each new person is related and why it may be enjoyable to spend time with them.

Chapter 4

Dealing With Ongoing Concerns

D uring a separation or divorce, many issues need to be resolved. Once there is a resolution, families may experience a sense of relief and a need to move on. Some issues linger, however, and are an ongoing source of concern and strain for the family. It is important to acknowledge and deal with these more subtle issues.

Increased Family Responsibilities

Separation and divorce lead to a shift and increase in responsibilities for parents and children. The cost of relocation, the maintenance of two households and payments for legal services create financial pressures. Women previously not employed outside the home may find it necessary to work long hours. Should remarriage occur, men may find themselves supporting two sets of children. In spite of long work hours, one or both parents may find it difficult or impossible to maintain a satisfactory standard of living.

When full-time employment is necessary, the issue of adequate supervision of children becomes a primary concern. Older children may spend a great deal of time alone or caring for younger siblings. In the absence of a second parent, household chores must be divided among family members and may need to be performed during leisure time, leaving few opportunities for recreation or relaxation.

School responsibilities become more complex for children because they have less parental supervision at home. The problem is compounded when children move back and forth from one home to another and must remember books, homework, gym equipment, and notes.

TASKS

1. If, because of limited finances, your child expresses a sense of deprivation, recognize that:

   • Particularly in our culture, the giving of material goods signifies caring. Your child may misinterpret your inability to give "things" as a sign of withdrawal of your affection. Reassure your child that this is not the case, and, whenever possible, demonstrate your caring in ways that do not cost money.

   • Children want material goods to gain acceptance from their peers. Help your child measure his self-worth by means other than outward appearances. Offer assistance in selecting purchases and finding ways to earn extra money.

2. Teach your child how to handle emergencies when you are not home. Look for structured activities to occupy your child while you work, or locate families your child can stay with when you are gone.

3. Do not let guilt, protectiveness, or a lack of assertiveness prevent you from asking your child to assume responsibility in the home. When you refrain from asking for help, frustration and anger build, with harmful effects on your relationship.

   • Develop and put in writing an organized system and schedule of chores for each family member. Include your child in decision making about who will do what and when. If, for instance, your child dislikes feeding the dog but would be willing to walk him instead, compromise is possible. Your child will be more cooperative having participated in planning her system of responsibilities.

- Maintain realistic expectations of your child. Does your child really have the ability and coordination to perform particular tasks to your satisfaction? You may need to lower your standards or find a more suitable task.

- Be clear about the rewards and consequences for completing a job. You might provide an allowance, a portion of which is earned for each job done. Perhaps the most effective reward, particularly with a young child, is to use extra time that results from sharing household responsibilities as special time for you and your child to share.

- Every few weeks re-evaluate the system with your child. Be willing to make reasonable changes.

4. Whenever possible, avoid using an older child as a parent substitute for a younger sibling. An older child excessively involved with child care may lack adequate time for academic, social, or recreational outlets. A younger child will miss the nurturing and supervision of an adult figure. The frustration that result from this arrangement can lead to increased sibling rivalry and conflict.

5. On the other hand, don't be afraid to ask your older child to provide child care in moderation. This arrangement can enhance the child's sense of responsibility and closeness with his sibling.

6. Develop an organized system that allows you to help your child with her school work. Help keep your child's belongings organized during changes from one household to another. Consult with your child's teachers so that they can be supportive.

7. Above all, do not be overly demanding of yourself or your child, especially during the early stages of separation and divorce. Stress and

life's many pressures make it impossible to be super-chef, super-housecleaner, super-student, super-employee, and super-parent. Be patient with yourself and your child during this period of adjustment. Set priorities and keep trying. Accept the fact that everything will not get done!

Loneliness

Loneliness accompanies the insecurity that surrounds a family change. Children wonder where they belong. Do they have a family to share with, belong to, learn from? Often children adjusting to separation and divorce perceive themselves as different from other children and their families. They may feel alienated from their peers, and this bewilderment and alienation lead to loneliness.

Another source of loneliness is the increased amount of time children spend alone. The majority of parents work, and their children are part of the "latch key" population. They may come home and stay alone or take care of younger children, thus spending less time with their friends.

Finally, loneliness comes when children miss their parent—-when one parent is away from home and the other parent has infrequent contact with the child.

TASKS

1. Set aside consistent sharing times, even if the actual amount of time is very small.

2. Familiarize yourself with community activities and their times and locations. Allow your child to choose at least one activity that interests her. For older children, encourage your child to make calls to get accurate information about activities. This will reinforce her sense of responsibility and commitment.

3. Use neighbors, singles' organizations, and other community organizations to meet the needs of different family members. For example, being part of a network may help you find transportation to an activity for your child while you are at work.

4. If you are away frequently, enroll your child in a survival skills course. You will feel more comfortable about safety, and your child will learn new ways to constructively use his time.

5. Share time and activities with other families who have experienced a family change. Companionship reduces feelings of isolation and reinforces the idea that you are a family, will survive, and can enjoy yourselves.

6. Spend time with other adults in order to reduce your sense of loneliness. In a couples-oriented society, it is difficult to be single. This is why singles organizations and support groups are so important. Your efforts to seek satisfying experiences will serve as an excellent model for your child.

Worries About the Future

Most children worry about the future. Younger children tend to be anxious about everyday, concrete concerns and routines, such as who will be there for them at lunch time and where they will sleep.

Older children worry about who will take care of them if something happens to one or both parents; how they will have enough money to go to school or to buy nice clothes; and finally, if they will be able to have a serious relationship or satisfying marriage.

TASKS

1. Discuss divorce-related facts with your child. If your child expresses concerns about what would happen to her in the event of your death, discuss the arrangements that have been made.

2. Ask your child how he feels about these arrangements.

3. It is important to be realistic about money. You may need to explain your limits on spending. However, do not overburden your child with details about finances and adult worries. If you and your former spouse have conflicts about money, make it clear to your child that it is a

parental problem. Above all, reassure your child that she will be cared for and that you have adults to turn to for assistance as needed.

4. Discuss the topic of relationships with your child. Talking about your own marriage can be an educational and sharing experience for both of you. Depending upon the age of your child, such a discussion might include:

    -   How you met and what you did
    -   How you communicated
    -   How you made decisions about money, family, children, leisure, careers, and chores
    -   How your family felt about your marriage
    -   How you fought and resolved differences
    -   How you shared significant happy and sad events during your life together
    -   How you each changed over the years and how these changes affected your marriage
    -   What you learned from your marriage

    A gentle, honest discussion along these lines teaches children about aspects of a relationship that affect the degree of satisfaction each partner experiences.

Chapter 5

Building a Network of Support

How well a family adapts to separation and divorce depends not only on its inner resources but on the support it receives from family and friends. Unfortunately, family and social ties frequently suffer as a result of separation or divorce. Friends of family may side with one spouse. Some friends may feel uncomfortable socializing with a single adult or a single-parent family. Newly single parents may be reluctant to pursue activities in which they previously took part as a couple. Household moves, near or far, create a barrier of distance that make it hard to maintain relationships. Living in a new neighborhood may mean living among strangers. Particularly in the beginning stages of adjustment to separation and divorce, the single parent may lack the time or energy to nurture old relationships or create new ones.

Families adjusting to separation and divorce frequently ask, "Who can I turn to for help and support?" Most people are trained to be problem solvers and consider themselves to be self-reliant. However, whether divorce is mutually initiated or not, most individuals still experience a "roller coaster" of emotions and can benefit greatly from the support of others. Seeking support from friends, relatives and/or professionals means that you are taking care of yourself and your children, and that you understand that you cannot expect yourself to have all the answers. Here are some suggestions to help you build a network of support:

TASKS

1. Make a special effort to involve yourself and your child in social, recreational and educational activities. If people seem too busy to get to know you, don't give up. Keep trying! Eventually, you and your child will find people who share your interests and who are interested in building relationships.

2. Look into joining a baby-sitting or child care cooperative. If none is available, try starting one in your neighborhood. You and your child will have an opportunity to become close to other people, and you will have another option for child care.

3. If you are feeling emotionally cut off from friends and relatives but would like to improve these relationships, make an extra effort to renew contact. Let your relatives and friends know that you want to maintain relationships that are meaningful to you and your child, and are willing to forget any ill feelings or discomfort caused by your separation or divorce.

4. Try reaching out and helping others. This will bring you personal satisfaction, and you will be more likely to enjoy favors from others in return.

5. Explore the different singles' organizations in your community and participate in the activities they offer. Pursue a personal interest and enjoy the company of people who share your interests. Don't worry about finding Mr. or Ms. "Right." Some singles' organizations also offer activities for families. These activities are one good way for kids to meet other kids from single-parent homes—something that is particularly important if you are new in town.

6. Don't expect to find all the things you like in one person. Different relationships have different purposes. One friend might be good for playing tennis with, another for dining out, and a third for sharing intimate feelings.

7. Remember, you have the power to control relationships. You can encourage or discourage people from getting close to you. Don't be discouraged if your efforts do not succeed immediately. Keep trying.

What kinds of support are there?

- Educational
- Legal
- Religious
- Support Groups
- Mediation
- Financial Planning
- Psychological Counseling
- Social
- Divorce Education Seminars

How to access support

- Educational: call the Board of Education in your school district ; speak to the school counselor, social worker or psychologist in your child's school.

- Financial: contact financial planners; call the Office of Child Support Enforcement or Social Services offices in your county.

- Legal: call the American Bar Association or your local Family Law section of the Bar Association.

- Libraries: investigate sections devoted to books for children and adults about coping with divorce.

- Psychological: call your local Mental Health Association or your health insurance company for referrals.

- Religious: call your local church or synagogue to inquire about pastoral counseling and support groups.

- Social: call single parent organizations to find out about their services.

Chapter 6

Taking the Next Steps

C hildren often remember their parents' relationships at its end, when there are tensions and conflicts. Their understanding of relationships becomes limited to the last events they witnessed. These events then become the "reasons" for the divorce in the childrens' eyes: "My father was a workaholic; my mother had an affair."

When parents and children can sit down together and share the development of the marital relationship, they build a foundation for understanding present friendships and forming future loving relationships. They see that there were once happy times and that there are different ways of solving marital problems. Such a discussion gives children a sense of hope about their own future relationships. When parents divorce in constructive ways and parent to meet their children's needs, children learn that they can survive difficult family changes and continue to have loving parent-child relationships.

We hope that by defining common problems and offering specific suggestions, we can help you and your child make the adjustment to divorce a process of growth. By coping constructively with family change, you and your child can enhance your understanding of yourselves and each other and grow closer through your ability to communicate and problem solve.

Parents and children seek some form of counseling for support, for help in making change, and most of all, to feel better. In an unconditionally accepting setting, it is often very helpful to see that you are not alone, have the opportunity to connect with others, and deal with issues that may not have surfaced or been resolved. Some parents and children are involved in counseling because they are in the midst of grief and need support to move forward and feel better. Other parents may want to further understand their role in the marriage and what happened that led to divorce. Parents may want to focus on what will be a healthy relationship for them in the future and parenting skills to enhance their parent-child relationship.

Children, in working with a clinician, learn to label and express their feelings, disengage from ongoing parent conflict, and discuss ways to move forward with aspects of their lives that they can control.

Group counseling can be beneficial to children and parents. Being in a group with others who are going through or have gone through a family transition helps group members to see that they are not alone; builds a support system that can extend beyond the group and provides a safe confidential arena in which one can learn from others and practice making constructive changes.

When Do I Know if My Children Need Help?

First and foremost, try to think preventively. Children can benefit from an opportunity to learn how to get in touch with their emotions and express them in healthy ways. When children understand what is happening in their worlds, and separate situations that they cannot control from those that they can, they maintain and enhance a sense of hope about their own lives.

There are some significant "signs" that parents and educators should always be aware of. It is important for your children and teens to seek help:

- When they feel sad for long periods of time and nothing seems to help them feel better:
  - they think more about the past more than the present
  - they cry over the littlest and biggest things and can't seem to stop

- they can't stop thinking about their parents' divorce
- they have little or no interest in playing or being with friends

- When they feel hopeless, have no goals and feel like they have no family and friends to support and help:
  - they wake up, but don't want to get up
  - they don't eat or they eat a lot when they are not hungry
  - they don't laugh, joke or enjoy anything that they are doing
  - they want to stay alone all the time

- When they don't have family and friends they can trust:
  - they believe that their parent(s) have not been honest with them
  - they don't think their friends can keep their confidence
  - they don't want to burden friends

- When they feel "stuck":
  - they believe that they are responsible for a parent or younger sibling
  - they feel caught in the middle of parents' arguing
  - they have difficulty communicating with a parent.

- When they feel angry all the time:
  - they take their anger out on innocent people
  - they act out with teachers and other people in authority
  - they fight with brothers, sisters or friends

- When they worry excessively:
  - they worry about their parents
  - they are extremely anxious when their parent is not physically with them
  - they worry about their own physical and psychological well-being

The following statements come from kids about talking to counselors, therapists, clergy and other helping professionals:

" It's important to go to a counselor when you feel you can't talk to anyone else."

" When you feel confused and emotionally mixed up, it's good to talk to a counselor."

" It's really necessary for everyone because everyone has emotions especially after a divorce. Kids may not know what they're feeling and counseling can help them get in touch with their feelings."

"I wish I had a counselor when I was a teen. I thought I was the only one whose parents divorced, and I never could share my feelings until now when I'm in my twenties. What torture!

Finally, a lot of parents wonder how effective mental health treatment is. Some questions to explore in answering are:

- How is my youngster participating in school, with friends and peers?
- How is my child following rules?
- Have there been any improvements? What are they?
- How has our relationship changed, and how is it with the other parents?

Creating Networks of Support

During one of the most difficult times in a family's life, adjusting to divorce also means learning to cope with changing support systems. Along with the losses involved in accepting that your expectations of marriage were not met, there are financial, psychological and social losses. Couple friends suddenly seem uncomfortable for you and for them; in-laws and biological parents may take sides; close friends tell you everything will be alright when that is the last thing you want to hear. Perhaps what distinguishes divorce from other family transitions is the loss of support and additional pressures in just about every aspect of life.

How, then, can you handle everything and make decisions that will impact you and your child for the rest of your lives? Don't do it alone!!! Many adults and children adjusting to divorce have to learn how to reach out and ask for support or help. That might mean changing how you think about asking for help. Accepting that you can't do it all alone and that you need support in various areas is a sign of strength. Remembering that you are a model for your child means you're demonstrating that it is okay to seek support outside the family.

FamilyConnex™

Helping Parents Choose a Family Focused Model of Decision Making

Becoming a single parent adds more hours, activities, tasks and demands. However, the time that parents spend with their children offers a wonderful opportunity to help loving relationships between parents and children. Regardless of parents' marital status, **FamilyConnex™ helps parents develop a civil, constructive co-parent relationship.**

This program teaches the information needed to create a child-focused, parent-initiated parent agreement. The self-paced program includes a comprehensive 35 page manual, information to be included in parenting agreements, and helpful tools to assist parents in building child-focused parenting plans for each child in their family.

$99.99   >Individual Subscription

Includes one proprietary username and password with full access to the needs assessment, online parenting agreement program, and parenting manual.

$149.99   >Co-Parent Subscription

Includes a proprietary username and password for each parent with full access to the needs assessment, online parenting agreement program, and parenting manual with no expiration date. Price the program as you wish or provide it as a complimentary service to your clients.

For more information, visit our website:

http://www.familyconnex.org

301-384-0079 or 410-740-9553

Mission Statement

The National Family Resiliency Center Inc. (NFRC) is committed to helping children and adults preserve a sense of family, foster healthy relationships, and adjust constructively to change, especially during times of separation, divorce, and other family transitions.

How Mission is Accomplished

Through a combination of professional clinical intervention services, peer counseling, community outreach and educational programs, research efforts, and opportunities for professional development, NFRC facilitates the development and maintenance of healthy and productive lifestyles.

As a private, non-profit organization, NFRC is an advocate and liaison for families in transition. The model of prevention and support plays an important role in the formation of nuclear family and community partnerships.

Individual and Family Therapy
- Individual Therapy
- Family Therapy
- Couple Counseling
- Co-Parent Counseling
- Pre-Marital & Marriage Counseling

Therapy Groups
- **Younger Elementary Aged Groups**
  Children in grades 1&2 meet in groups of six to work on divorce related issues through play, activities and discussion. Weekly groups include participation by parents.

- **Elementary Aged Groups**
  Children in grades 3-5 learn techniques for identifying concerns, labeling and expressing feelings, problem solving and effective communication around divorce related issues. Parents are closely involved through individual and multiple family sessions.

- **Middle School Aged Groups**
  Children in grades 6-8 meet weekly to identify feelings related to divorce, do specific family problem solving and gain skills to communicate with parents & peers. Parents involved through individual and multiple family sessions.

- **High School Aged Group**
  Provides an opportunity for teens in grades 9-12 to explore and resolve divorce related concerns, as well as an opportunity to focus on many issues such as dating and decisions about college, friendships, etc. Teens connect about how comfortable it is to talk and be understood by their peers. Parents join at end in multiple family groups.

- **Adult Women's and Men's Support Groups**
  Provides support and resources to adults in phases of adjustment to separation and divorce.

Educational Programs

- **Healing Hearts:** Regaining a Sense of Family after Transitions. Two, three-hour seminars offer parents strategies to help themselves and their children cope with family transitions.
- **Kidshare: A Special Time for Kids and Teens to Learn about Separation and Divorce**
  Two, two-hour, age appropriate programs for children and teens provides youth with an opportunity to understand some of the changes taking place in their family and learn to identify feelings, solve problems and gain a sense of hope for themselves and their families.

The National Family Resiliency Program

The National Family Resiliency Center, Inc.(NFRC) has worked with more than 18,000 individuals since 1981. The National Family Resiliency Program® informs parents and professionals about alternatives to the traditional adversarial process of divorce and offers a menu of comprehensive services provided by a multi-disciplinary team of professionals including judges, attorneys, mediators, educators and mental health professionals. The National Family Resiliency Program is a state of the art program which focuses parents' attention on the needs of each of their children and offers parents a healthier process of separation and divorce, one which takes into consideration the psychological, financial and legal aspects of a family transition.

As part of the National Family Resiliency Program, NFRC staff offers three publications for families experiencing a transition. The books: *Snowman* (a story for younger children), *A Kids Guide to Separation and Divorce* (for older children) and *Stop! In the Name of Love for Your Children* (for parents) were written by judges, attorneys, mediators and mental health professionals. The book for parents explains options available, which encourage a non-adversarial divorce as well as specific strategies to help their children cope. The children's books offer support and hope for children who may feel confused and sad about their families' separation.

In addition to the direct services offered at our center in Maryland, the NFRC professional training staff offer consultation and training for judges, attorneys, guardians *ad litem*, mediators, educators and mental health professionals who are interested in implementing the National Family Resiliency Program in their community. As a systems reform initiative, the National Family Resiliency program offers a wellness model for communities and court systems that focuses on encouraging healthy parental decision making, reducing the amount of litigation surrounding decisions about children and strengthening families.

For information on professional training, contact The National Family Resiliency Program at 410-740-9553 or email us at sales@divorceabc.com or visit us on our website at www.divorceABC.com.